KU-557-832

Schools Library and Information Services
S00000797344

By

Steffi Cavell-Clarke

©2017
Book Life
King's Lynn
Norfolk PE30 4LS

ISBN: 978-1-78637-150-8

Printed in Malaysia

Written by:
Steffi Cavell-Clarke

Edited by:
Charlie Ogden

Designed by:
Danielle Jones

A catalogue record for this book is available from the British Library

PHOTO CREDITS

Abbreviations: l-left, r-right, b-bottom, t-top, c-centre, m-middle.

Front cover – Elena Elisseeva, Monkey Business Images, kzww, italianestro, Zoom Team, GongTo. 1 – italianestro. 2– Sunny studio. 3– Elena Elisseeva. 4 – Romolo Tavani 4br – GongTo. 5r – amenic181 5tm – Dean Fikar 5m – Monkey Business Images 5bm – alsem 5lm – Elena Elisseeva. 6 main: Thammanoon Khamchalee 6br – Yellow Cat. 7main – Romas_Photo 7tl – Alinute Silzeviciute 7ml – gorillaimages 7bl – Romas_Photo. 8l – Nataliia Melnychuk 8r – Vitalina Rybakova 8m – Palokha Tetiana 8bm – Praisaeng. 9main – Nataliia Melnychuk 9tl – graletta 9m - sharshonm 9ml – Africa Studio 9bl – oksana2010. 10 main – Krasowit 10m – mayakova 10b – Abel Tumik. 11main – sayhmog 11tl – Stephanie Frey 11ml – Zeljko Radojko 11l – Tarica. 12 – Hriana. 13main – FreeBirdPhotos 13tl – Brian A Jackson 13bl – Barbol. 14main – By U. S. Fish and Wildlife Service - Northeast Region [CC BY 2.0 (http://creativecommons.org/licenses/by/2.0)], via Wikimedia Commons. 15main – amenic181 15tl – KULISH VIKTORIIA 15m – Natalia Paklina 15ml – Perutskyi Petro 15bl – Singkham. 16main – Robert Przybysz 16mr – Ev. Safronov. 17main - tongo51 17tl – Zoom Team 17 ml – popular business 17 bl – tongo51. 18 – Alena Brozova. 19 – Katrina Leigh. 20main – Yorkman 20mr – Tatyana Vyc. 21main – hurricanehank 21tl – GOLFX 21ml – ampol sonthong 21bl – macknimal. 22main – Santhosh Varghese 22br – Richard Griffin. 23main – Diana Taliun 23tl – VAV 23ml – Irina Bg 23bl – Pavel Kobysh. Images are courtesy of Shutterstock.com. With thanks to Getty Images, Thinkstock Photo and iStockphoto.

plant parts

Seeds

CONTENTS

Add Sunshine

Words that look like **this** can be found in the glossary on page 24.

What Is a Plant?

A plant is a living thing. All living things need water, air and sunlight to live.

There are many different kinds of plant. Most plants have roots, leaves, flowers and a stem.

Plants live all around the world!

What Is a Seed?

A seed is made by a fully-grown plant.
A plant usually makes lots of seeds.

A seed can grow into a new plant. It needs water, warmth and sunlight to grow.

What Do Seeds Look Like?

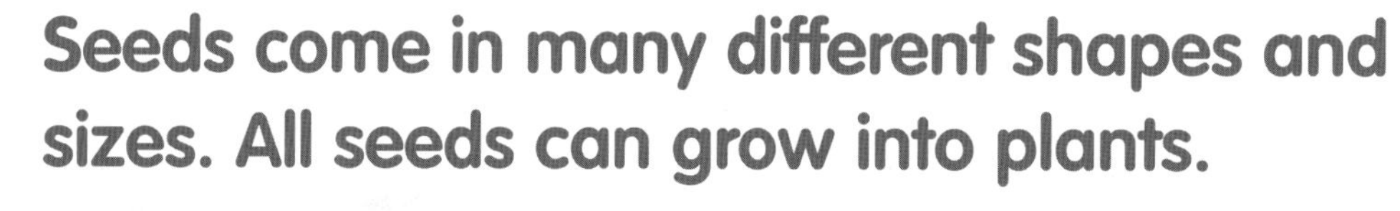

Seeds come in many different shapes and sizes. All seeds can grow into plants.

A seed usually has a hard shell, which protects it until it is ready to grow.

Horse chestnut seeds have spiky shells!

Where Do Seeds Come From?

Seeds can also grow inside fruit, like apples.

A seed usually comes from a plant's flowers.

The centre of a sunflower head is made up of lots of tiny flowers that all turn into seeds.

Seeds on the Move

Seeds usually move away from the plant that they grew on as this gives them the best chance of survival.

Some seeds are blown away by the wind and become buried in soil.

A dandelion flower uses the wind to move its seeds.

Some seeds grow inside fruit or berries. When birds eat fruit or berries, they eat the seeds too.

The bird will then fly away and poo the seeds out somewhere else!

The seeds will still be able to grow!

What Do Seeds Need?

Most seeds need to be buried in soil for them to grow. They also need water and sunlight.

Once the seed has everything it needs, its hard shell will split open and a new plant will begin to grow.

How Do Seeds Grow?

As the seed splits open, roots begin to grow downwards and a tiny shoot begins to grow upwards.

Shoot
Soil
Root
Seed

Seeds in the Greenhouse

A greenhouse is a glass building where people can grow their own plants. Greenhouses can stay warm even in cold weather.

Many different types of seed can be planted in a greenhouse and kept warm.

A gardener can water the seeds to help them to grow.

Tasty Seeds

There are many different types of seed that humans can eat. Lots of these seeds can be eaten as a healthy snack!

Peas are seeds that come out of their own little pod.
Pea Pod

GLOSSARY

grow	naturally develop and increase in size
protects	looks after and keeps safe
soil	the upper layer of earth where plants grow
sunlight	light from the sun
survival	continuing to stay alive

INDEX

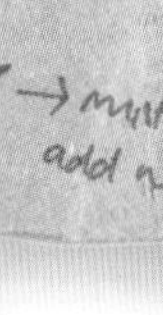